D0696912

meals like mom used to make

# Meals Like MOM used to make

## karen brown

*Dinner Menus & Recipes from Days Gone By*

THE SUMMIT GROUP
FORT WORTH, TEXAS

THE SUMMIT GROUP
1227 West Magnolia, Suite 500, Fort Worth, Texas, 76104

Copyright © 1993 by The Summit Group. All rights reserved. No part of this book may be reproduced or transmitted in any form or by any means, electronic or mechanical, including photocopying, recording or by any information storage and retrieval system, without the written permission of the publisher, except where permitted by law.

*Publisher's Cataloging in Publication*

Brown, Karen.
  Meals like Mom used to make : complete dinner menus and recipes
  from days gone by/Karen Brown.
  p. cm.
  Includes index.
  ISBN 1-56530-049-1

  1. Cookery, American. 2. Menus. I. Title.

TX715.B77 1993            641.5'973
                          QBI93-681

Jacket design by Rishi Seth
Book design by Rishi Seth
Cover Photograph of head and hands by Archive Photos/Lambert
Hand-tinted by Leslie Fratkin

Manufactured in the United States of America
First Printing 1993

To my mother, Betty Lancaster, the ultimate mom.

# Contents

# *Introduction*

Are you longing for '50s food—the pot roasts, chicken and dumplings, and apple pies of your childhood—the meals just like your mom used to make?

When my son was born, I wanted to pass on to him some of the values and traditions that were a part of my childhood—and one of those traditions was wholesome, home-cooked food. That's when I began collecting the recipes that make up this book.

They are organized into menus to make meal-planning easy and, perhaps, to remind you of some combinations of dishes from your own childhood.

I hope you enjoy the cookbook and wish you many happy mealtimes.

Family dinners around the table make for good meals and great memories. For busy families on the run, though, scheduling regular dinners can be a challenge. I know of one family whose idea of a seated dinner is when they're all sitting together in the car as it drives through the local fast-food spot! But there is a way that you can help bring back some of the traditions you enjoyed as a child—by scheduling special mealtimes with your family, even if it's only once a week. Let them know that this time has been set aside for a dinner with the television turned off, and a chance for lots of conversation and verbal "catch-up"—all centered around a delicious, home-style meal. The main point is that this is a family time, a time for participation, communication and just plain old togetherness.

# Menu 1

meat loaf

mashed potatoes

baked squash

carrot-raisin salad

whole wheat rolls

banana pudding

# meat loaf

*2 pounds ground chuck*
*1 can tomato soup*
*1 cup bread crumbs*
*1 green pepper, chopped*
*1 onion, chopped*
*1 egg, slightly beaten*
*1 teaspoon Worcestershire sauce*
*1¹/₂ teaspoons salt*
*¹/₂ teaspoons pepper*

Mix all ingredients, form into a loaf and place in baking pan. Bake at 350 degrees for one-and-a-half hours. During last half-hour, top with sauce. Serves 6 to 8.

*Sauce:*
*1 can tomato soup*
*3 tablespoons brown sugar*
*2 tablespoons prepared mustard*
*3 tablespoons vinegar*
*2 teaspoons Worcestershire sauce*

Combine all ingredients and pour over meat loaf.

# mashed potatoes

*4 medium potatoes*
*3 tablespoons butter or margarine*
*¹/₄ cup milk*
*Salt and pepper to taste*

Peel, slice and boil potatoes until tender. Drain and add butter, milk, salt and pepper. Beat with electric mixer until smooth, adding more milk if desired. Serve at once. Serves 4.

# baked squash

*3 cups yellow squash, sliced*
*3 eggs, slightly beaten*
*¹/₄ cup milk*
*¹/₄ cup butter or margarine, melted*
*1 teaspoon salt*
*¹/₄ teaspoon pepper*
*¹/₂ cup bread crumbs*

Cook squash in small amount of water until tender. Drain and mash well with a fork. Combine all other ingredients, except bread crumbs, and fold in squash. Pour into greased casserole and top with bread crumbs. Bake at 350 degrees for 45 minutes. Serves 4.

# carrot-raisin salad

*2¹/₂ cups grated raw carrots*
*³/₄ cup seedless raisins*
*¹/₄ cup mayonnaise*

Combine carrots and raisins. Stir in mayonnaise, adding more if desired. Chill. Serves 4 to 6.

# whole wheat rolls

*2 yeast cakes*
*1¹/₄ cups milk, heated*
*¹/₃ cup oil*
*2 eggs, beaten*
*1 cup white flour*
*¹/₄ cup sugar*
*1 teaspoon salt*
*3 cups whole wheat flour*

Dissolve yeast in ¹/₄ cup of the warm milk. In mixing bowl, combine remaining 1 cup milk with oil, eggs and yeast mixture. Sift together white flour, sugar, and salt, and stir into milk mixture. Gradually stir in whole wheat flour until well mixed. Form into balls and place on greased cookie sheet to rise for 2 hours, or until double in size. Bake at 400 degrees for 15-20 minutes. Yields 2 dozen.

# banana pudding

*5 eggs*
*2 cups water*
*One 5-ounce can evaporated milk*
*1 tablespoon butter*
*2$^1$/$_2$ cups sugar*
*1 cup flour*
*5 ripe bananas, peeled and sliced*
*1 tablespoon vanilla*
*vanilla wafers*

In double boiler, mix eggs, water, milk and butter. Cook over medium heat. Sift together flour and sugar, and add to mixture, stirring constantly until thick. Remove from heat and fold in bananas and vanilla. Pour into dish lined with vanilla wafers. Add more wafers on top and serve warm or chilled. Serves 6 to 8.

# *Menu 2*

pot roast

with potatoes and carrots

bibb lettuce with cream
dressing

refrigerator yeast rolls

boston cream pie

Do you think June Cleaver would have served bean sprouts and tofu to the Beaver? Of course not! As we children of the '50s well know, the best moms provided their families with a lot of love, warmth—and great pot roast!

# pot roast with potatoes and carrots

*3-or 4-pound rump or round roast*
*3 tablespoons oil*
*1 teaspoon salt*
*½ teaspoon pepper*
*1 envelope dry onion soup mix*
*One 10-ounce can condensed beef consomme*
*½ cup water*
*2 potatoes, peeled and quartered*
*4 carrots, peeled and chopped*
*4 stalks celery, chopped*

Brown roast in hot oil. Place beef in large roasting pan and sprinkle with salt, pepper, and dry soup mix. Combine consomme and water, and pour over roast. Cover and bake at 350 degrees for 3 hours. During last hour of cooking time, add potatoes, carrots and celery.

This is even more tender when cooked in a crock pot. After browning beef in oil, place all ingredients in pot. (Use only ½ can of consomme and ¼ cup water.) Cook on low heat for 10-12 hours.

# bibb lettuce with cream dressing

$1/2$ cup heavy cream
2 tablespoons lemon juice
1 teaspoon salt
$1/4$ teaspoon pepper
3 tablespoons oil
3-4 heads Bibb lettuce

Beat together cream, lemon juice, salt and pepper until foamy. Stir in oil and chill. Tear lettuce into serving size pieces and toss with dressing.

# refrigerator yeast rolls

*4 tablespoons shortening*
*¼ cup sugar*
*1 teaspoon salt*
*1 cup scalded milk*
*1 package yeast*
*¼ cup lukewarm water*
*1 egg*
*3 to 3½ cups sifted flour*

Combine shortening, sugar and salt in milk. Heat and cool. Dissolve yeast in lukewarm water. Beat egg slightly with yeast mixture. Add to cooled milk. Mix in flour until dough is workable. Cover loosely with waxed paper and chill overnight. Roll and cut. Let rise on greased pan 1 to 1½ hours. Bake at 400 degrees for 12-15 minutes.

To freeze, bake for only 8 minutes. Cool, wrap well and freeze. To serve, place frozen rolls in 400-degree oven and bake until golden brown.

# boston cream pie

*Sponge Cake:*
*3 eggs*
*1 cup sugar*
*1 cup flour*
*1 teaspoon baking powder*
*1/2 teaspoon salt*
*1/3 cup milk, heated*
*1 teaspoon vanilla*

Beat eggs well (at least 3 minutes) and add sugar. Sift together flour, baking powder and salt, and fold into egg mixture. Stir in hot milk and vanilla, and pour into two greased, 9-inch cake pans. Bake at 375 degrees for about 20 minutes, or until golden brown. Cool completely before removing from pans.

*Cream Filling:*
*1 1/4 cups cream*
*1/2 cup sugar*
*1/4 cup flour*
*3 egg yolks, beaten*
*2 teaspoons vanilla*

Scald cream. In top of double boiler, over hot water, combine sugar, flour and egg yolks, stirring constantly until thick. Add scalded cream and vanilla, and bring to a boil. Remove from heat and cool.

*Chocolate Glaze:*
*1/4 cup cream*
*2 ounces chocolate*
*3 tablespoons butter*
*1 1/2 cups powdered sugar*

Heat cream. Melt together chocolate and butter. Stir sugar into cream and add chocolate mixture. Beat by hand until smooth. Spread cream filling between the two cake layers and spread chocolate glaze on top layer. Chill and serve.

# Menu 3

baked ham

cheese grits

lima beans

hot curried fruit

buttermilk biscuits

peach cobbler

# baked ham

*6-to 8-pound fully cooked, boneless ham*
*whole cloves*
*1 cup brown sugar*
*1 cup dark corn syrup*
*2 tablespoons prepared mustard*
*1 teaspoon lemon juice*

Place ham in roasting pan and insert meat thermometer. Bake at 325 degrees for 2 to 2½ hours, or until thermometer indicates ham is at 130 degrees.

Remove ham from oven, remove thermometer and make shallow, diagonal criss-cross cuts in the fat along the top of the ham, forming a grid-like pattern. Push a clove into each diamond shape. Mix together brown sugar, corn syrup, mustard and lemon juice, and pour on top of ham. Adjust oven temperature up to 400 degrees and return ham to oven for 10 minutes, or until glaze is golden.

# cheese grits

*1 cup quick-cooking grits*
*1 cup grated cheddar cheese*
*1 clove garlic, minced*
*1 stick butter or margarine*
*1 teaspoon salt*
*½ teaspoon pepper*
*2 eggs, beaten*
*¾ cup milk*

Cook grits according to package directions. Add cheese, garlic, butter, salt and pepper, and mix well. Cool. Combine eggs and milk, and fold into grits mixture. Pour into greased casserole and bake, uncovered, at 375 degrees for one hour. Serves 6-8.

# lima beans

*1 pound lima beans, shelled*
*1 teaspoon salt*
*½ teaspoon pepper*
*3 tablespoons butter or margarine*

Place beans in enough boiling salted water to cover. Cook, covered, over low heat for one hour, or until tender. Season with salt, pepper, and butter. Serves 6-8.

# hot curried fruit

*One 1-pound can seedless tart cherries*
*One 1-pound can sliced pears*
*One 1-pound can pineapple chunks*
*One 1-pound can mandarin oranges*
*1 cup brown sugar*
*$1/2$ cup orange juice*
*1 stick butter or margarine*
*2 teaspoons curry powder*
*1 teaspoon ground ginger*

Drain fruit and slice into smaller pieces if desired. In saucepan over low heat, mix together brown sugar, orange juice, butter, curry powder and ginger. Place fruit in large, greased casserole and pour sauce over all. Bake at 325 degrees for one hour and serve warm. Serves 10-12.

# buttermilk biscuits

*2 cups sifted flour*
*1 1/2 teaspoons baking powder*
*1/2 teaspoon soda*
*1 teaspoon salt*
*1/2 cup shortening*
*2/3 cup buttermilk*

Sift together flour, baking powder, soda and salt. Using two knives or pastry blender, cut in shortening. Stir in buttermilk and knead lightly on floured surface. Roll out to 1/4 inch thickness and cut with a 2 to 3 inch biscuit cutter. Let set for a few minutes before baking at 450 degrees for 10-12 minutes. Yields approximately 1 dozen.

# peach cobbler

*½ stick butter*
*½ cup all-purpose flour*
*½ cup sugar*
*1 teaspoon baking powder*
*½ cup milk*
*One 29-ounce can sliced peaches*

Chop butter into small pieces and place in bottom of 10-inch square baking dish. Combine flour, sugar and baking powder. Stir in milk until well mixed and pour into pan, on top of butter. Spoon peaches into pan, allowing space for the batter to bubble through during baking. (The crust will rise through to the top.) Bake at 350 degrees for 1 hour. Serve warm with ice cream. Serves 6-8.

# Menu 4

roast turkey

with cornbread dressing

giblet gravy

sweet potato soufflé

cranberry salad

refrigerator yeast rolls

pumpkin pie

Remember the Thanksgiving dinners of your childhood, when your mom and grandmother would put in an 18-hour day prior to the BIG DINNER EVENT? Well, you can still have those wonderful, traditional dishes without all of the effort: most of the recipes on this menu can be made ahead of time and frozen. And now, due to advanced techniques, turkeys are super easy to prepare.

# roast turkey

For easiest preparation, purchase a frozen, butter-basted
turkey. Allow 2-3 days for thawing in your refrigerator,
and remove giblets from the neck and body cavities, set-
ting them aside for giblet gravy.

Line a shallow roasting pan with foil. Place the turkey in
the pan, breast side up. Cover with pieces of aluminum
foil, sealing the top to form a loose tent around the bird.
Bake at 325 degrees.

*Cooking times:*
*4-8 pounds: 2 to 3 hours*
*8-12 pounds: $2^{1}/_{2}$ to $4^{1}/_{2}$ hours*
*12-16 pounds: $3^{1}/_{2}$ to $4^{1}/_{2}$ hours*
*16-20 pounds: $4^{1}/_{2}$ to $5^{1}/_{2}$ hours*

During the last hour of cooking time, remove top foil
pieces to allow the turkey to brown. Test for how well
done by lifting gently on the drumstick—when it pulls
away easily, it's done. (Or purchase a turkey equipped
with a built-in thermometer to let you know when it's
ready.)

# cornbread dressing

Bake the cornbread first. (Or use one of the good cornbread mixes on the market—double the recipe.)

*Cornbread (a double recipe):*
*2 eggs, beaten*
*2 cups milk*
*6 tablespoons oil*
*2 cups cornmeal*
*2 cups flour*
*8 teaspoons baking powder*
*1 teaspoon soda*
*2 teaspoons salt*
*4 teaspoons sugar*

Mix eggs, milk and oil. Sift together dry ingredients and pour into egg mixture, mixing until slightly lumpy. Pour into a greased 9x13-inch pan and bake at 400 degrees for 20-30 minutes, or until golden brown.

### Cornbread Dressing continued

*Dressing:*
*8 stalks celery, chopped*
*2 onions, chopped*
*1½ sticks butter or margarine*
*cornbread (double recipe)*
*4 slices bread, white or wheat*
*4 eggs*
*2 tablespoons parsley*
*2 teaspoons black pepper*
*1 tablespoon sage*
*2 teaspoons salt*
*2 tablespoons Worcestershire sauce*
*1 cup canned chicken broth (or turkey juice)*

Sauté celery and onion in butter until tender. In large mixing bowl, crumble together cornbread and bread slices. Combine eggs with spices, Worcestershire sauce and broth. Pour over bread crumbs and add cooked celery and onion, mixing until smooth. Use to stuff turkey or place in greased 10x14-inch pan and bake uncovered at 400 degrees for 30-40 minutes, or until lightly browned. May be frozen prior to baking. Serves 8 to 10.

# giblet gravy

*turkey giblets*
*4 tablespoons butter*
*4 tablespoons flour*
*1 teaspoon salt*
*$^1$/$_2$ teaspoon pepper*
*2 cups pan drippings from turkey (or canned chicken broth)*
*$^1$/$_2$ cup milk or cream*
*2 hardboiled eggs, chopped*

Wash the giblets and cover with water in small saucepan. Bring to a boil and simmer until tender. Drain, cool and chop into small pieces. Melt the butter in a skillet. Brown the flour in the melted butter, and add salt and pepper. Mix in drippings or broth, then add milk, stirring until thick. Add cooked eggs and giblet pieces. Serve over turkey and dressing.

# sweet potato soufflé

*One 29-ounce can sweet potatoes, drained*
*1 cup brown sugar*
*2 eggs, slightly beaten*
*1 cup milk*
*1 stick butter, melted*
*1 teaspoon vanilla*
*1 teaspoon cinnamon*
*$1/2$ teaspoon nutmeg*
*marshmallows*

Whip together all ingredients except marshmallows until smooth. Pour into greased casserole and top with marshmallows. Bake at 350 degrees for 30 minutes. Serves 6-8. Can be frozen prior to baking, but add marshmallows just before cooking.

# cranberry salad

*One 6-ounce package cherry gelatin*
*2 cups boiling water*
*One 16-ounce can whole-berry cranberry sauce*
*2 cups sour cream*
*1 cup miniature marshmallows*
*1 cup chopped pecans*

Stir gelatin into boiling water until dissolved and add cranberry sauce. Chill until thickening just begins. Fold in sour cream, marshmallows and pecans. Pour into greased, 2-quart mold and chill until completely set. Serves 10-12.

# refrigerator yeast rolls

(See p. 13)

# pumpkin pie

*3 eggs*
*One 1-pound can pumpkin*
*¹/₂ cup brown sugar*
*¹/₄ cup granulated sugar*
*1 teaspoon cinnamon*
*¹/₂ teaspoon salt*
*¹/₂ teaspoon ginger*
*¹/₂ teaspoon nutmeg*
*¹/₄ teaspoon cloves*
*1¹/₂ cups evaporated milk*
*1 teaspoon vanilla*
*9-inch unbaked pie shell*

In mixing bowl beat eggs. Continue beating and add pumpkin, sugars, salt and spices. Mix in milk and vanilla, and pour into pie shell. Bake at 350 degrees for 60-70 minutes, or until inserted knife comes out clean. Cool completely before slicing. Serve with sweetened whipped cream. Serves 8.

*Pie Crust:*
*1 cup all-purpose flour*
*$1/2$ teaspoon salt*
*$1/3$ heaping cup shortening*
*2 tablespoons ice water*

Sift together flour and salt in mixing bowl. With pastry blender or two knives, cut in shortening until grainy. Add the water and mix thoroughly. Knead lightly and roll out to circular shape on floured surface. Carefully fold pastry and place into 9-inch pie pan, crimping edges.

# *Menu 5*

swiss steak

macaroni and cheese

fried eggplant

waldorf salad

poppyseed bread

family-style bananas foster

A "must" for busy cooks, whether they work in or outside of the home, is the slow cooker. It adapts well to many recipes, like this Swiss steak. It takes just a few minutes to toss the ingredients into the crock pot in the morning (or the night before). And nothing is more comforting than arriving home after a long day with the aroma of your ready-to-eat dinner to greet you as you walk in the door.

# swiss steak

*2 pounds round steak*
*¹/₂ cup flour*
*2 teaspoons salt*
*¹/₂ teaspoon pepper*
*3 tablespoons oil*
*1 onion, chopped*
*2 stalks celery, chopped*
*2 carrots, peeled and sliced thin*
*2 teaspoons Worcestershire sauce*
*One 15-ounce can tomato sauce*
*One 16-ounce can beef broth*

Cut steak into serving-size pieces, trimming fat. Combine flour, salt and pepper, and coat steak pieces. Pound in flour with meat tenderizer. Brown steaks in hot oil, then drain grease. Add remaining ingredients and simmer, covered, on low heat for about two hours, or until tender, adding water if necessary. Serves 4-6.

This is delicious when done in a crock pot. Coat and brown steaks, then place on top of onion in pot. Top with remaining ingredients, eliminating beef broth. The additional liquids are unnecessary, as the meat will produce its own juices when cooked so slowly. Cook on low heat for 8-10 hours.

# macaroni and cheese

*½ cup butter or margarine*
*¼ cup flour*
*2½ cups milk*
*1 teaspoon salt*
*¼ teaspoon pepper*
*2 cups grated American cheese*
*2 cups elbow macaroni, cooked to yield 4 cups*

Melt butter in large skillet and stir in flour. Brown lightly and slowly add milk, stirring constantly. After sauce thickens, remove from heat and add salt, pepper and cheese. Carefully fold in cooked macaroni until it is well coated and pour into greased casserole. Bake at 350 degrees for 30 minutes. Serves 6 to 8.

# fried eggplant

*1 medium eggplant*
*lemon juice*
*2 eggs, slightly beaten*
*1 teaspoon salt*
*¼ teaspoon pepper*
*2 cups bread crumbs*
*3 tablespoons Parmesan cheese*
*½ cup oil*

Cut eggplant crosswise into very thin slices. Sprinkle lightly with lemon juice and set aside. Mix together eggs, salt and pepper. In separate dish, combine bread crumbs and Parmesan cheese. Dip eggplant slices first in egg mixture, then in crumb mixture to coat. Fry in hot oil for 5-6 minutes, turning to brown both sides. Serves 4-6.

# waldorf salad

*2 medium red apples*
*1 cup chopped celery*
*1/2 cup chopped walnuts*
*1/4 cup mayonnaise*
*1/4 teaspoon salt*
*lettuce leaves*

Peel and core apples; chop into small pieces. Mix together with remaining ingredients. Chill and serve on a lettuce leaf. Serves 4.

# poppyseed bread

*2 eggs*
*1 cup sugar*
*1/2 cup oil*
*1 cup evaporated milk*
*2 cups flour*
*2 teaspoons baking powder*
*1/2 teaspoon salt*
*1/4 cup poppy seeds*

Beat eggs, adding sugar, oil and milk. Sift together flour, baking powder and salt, and beat into egg mixture. Stir in poppy seeds and pour into greased 9x5-inch loaf pan. Bake at 350 degrees for 1 to 1 1/4 hours.

# family-style bananas foster

*4 tablespoons brown sugar*
*2 tablespoons butter*
*2 ripe bananas, peeled and sliced lengthwise*
*cinnamon*
*vanilla ice cream*

Melt sugar and butter. Add bananas and sauté until tender. Sprinkle with cinnamon and serve warm over vanilla ice cream. Serves 4.

Getting your family members involved in menu planning, grocery shopping, and the actual food preparation is a help for you, and gives everyone an opportunity for more interaction (and may help them to appreciate you a little more!). Send your teenagers to the grocery store with your food list (and a spending budget). And the little ones, especially, love to help. Let them grate cheese, measure ingredients, stir and mix, and you'll end up with an enthusiastic cook—and hopefully, a future kitchen helper.

# Menu 6

tuna-noodle casserole

sautéed snow peas

fruit salad with poppyseed
dressing

popovers

gingerbread

# tuna-noodle casserole

*One 10½-ounce can condensed cream of celery soup*
*½ cup milk*
*½ cup mayonnaise*
*1 cup grated cheddar cheese*
*1 cup chopped celery*
*¼ cup onion*
*¼ cup chopped green pepper*
*One 6-ounce package medium noodles, cooked and*
*    drained*
*One 12½-ounce can tuna*
*1 cup bread crumbs*

Combine soup, milk, mayonnaise and cheese. Add chopped vegetables, and fold in cooked noodles and drained tuna. Pour into greased casserole dish and top with bread crumbs. Bake at 350 degrees for 30 minutes, or until thoroughly heated. Serves 6 to 8.

# sautéed snow peas

*1 pound snow peas*
*2 tablespoons oil*
*salt*
*pepper*

Slice off ends of snow peas and pull off strings. Heat oil in
skillet over medium-high heat and add snow peas. Cook
and stir for about five minutes. Sprinkle with salt and
pepper, and serve warm. Serves 4.

# fresh fruit with poppyseed dressing

*1 apple*
*1 banana*
*1 orange*
*6 to 8 strawberries*
*lettuce leaves*

Peel and chop fruit into bite-size pieces. Chill. Serve on lettuce leaf with poppyseed dressing. Serves 4 to 6.

*Poppyseed Dressing:*
*1 cup oil*
*²/₃ cup sugar*
*¹/₃ cup vinegar*
*1¹/₂ teaspoon poppy seeds*
*1 teaspoon salt*

Mix together until smooth. Chill.

# popovers

*Butter*
*2 eggs*
*1 cup milk*
*1 cup sifted flour*
*1 teaspoon salt*

Liberally butter each muffin cup and place muffin tin in 425-degree oven until very hot. For batter, in large mixing bowl beat eggs and add milk. Sift together flour and salt, and add to egg mixture. Batter should be very thin. Pour into hot tins and bake for 25-30 minutes. Serve immediately with butter. Yields 8-10 popovers.

# gingerbread

*1 egg*
*½ cup sugar*
*½ cup butter, melted*
*2½ cups all-purpose flour*
*1½ teaspoons soda*
*1½ teaspoons ginger*
*1 teaspoon cinnamon*
*½ teaspoon salt*
*¼ teaspoon ground cloves*
*½ cup molasses*
*½ cup honey*
*1 cup boiling water*

Beat egg, adding sugar and butter. Sift together flour and other dry ingredients. Combine molasses, honey and boiling water until smooth, and blend into egg mixture. Combine with dry ingredients and pour into greased 9x9-inch pan. Bake at 350 degrees for 50-55 minutes. Cool completely and cut into squares. Serves 6 to 8.

# Menu 7

chicken pot pie

pear-cottage cheese salad

blueberry muffins

baked apples

Had your fill of fussy, trendy dishes—and unidentifiable food objects on your plate? Here's one back-to-the-basics meal from the heartland.

# chicken pot pie

*Filling:*
*3-4 pounds chicken pieces*
*3 cups milk*
*1 tablespoon butter*
*2 teaspoons salt*
*1 cup chicken stock*
*3 tablespoons cornstarch*
*One 10-ounce package frozen carrots*
*One 10-ounce package frozen peas*

Boil chicken until tender, about 1 hour. Drain, reserving chicken stock for crust and filling. Cool chicken, remove skin and bones, and chop meat into small pieces. Stir together milk, butter, salt and stock over medium heat. Add cornstarch and stir until thick. Fold in carrots and peas, and cook until tender. Add chicken and pour into prepared crust in 9x13-inch pan. Top with remaining crust and, if desired, brush top with beaten egg. Cut slits in top to vent. Bake at 400 degrees for 30 minutes, or until crust is golden brown and filling is bubbling. Serves 8 to 10.

*Crust:*
*3 cups flour*
*1 teaspoon baking powder*
*1 teaspoon salt*
*1 cup shortening*
*1 egg, slightly beaten*
*$^{1}/_{3}$ to $^{1}/_{2}$ cup chicken broth*

Sift together flour, baking powder, and salt and cut in shortening with two knives until grainy. Add egg and enough broth to moisten, and knead slightly on floured surface. Roll out two crusts, for top and bottom.

# pear-cottage cheese salad

*4 canned pear halves*
*4 lettuce leaves*
*1 pint cottage cheese*
*1 cup shredded cheddar cheese*

Drain and chill pear halves. Place on lettuce leaf and scoop $^{1}/_{2}$ cup cottage cheese onto center of each, sprinkling cheddar cheese on top. Serve cold. Serves 4.

# blueberry muffins

*1 egg, beaten*
*1 cup milk*
*¼ cup butter or margarine, melted*
*2 cups flour*
*⅓ cup sugar*
*1 tablespoon baking powder*
*½ teaspoon salt*
*1 cup blueberries, drained*

In mixing bowl, use fork to combine egg, milk and butter. Sift together flour, sugar, baking powder and salt, and combine with egg mixture. Fold in blueberries and spoon into well-greased muffin cups, ⅔ full. Bake at 425 degrees for 20 minutes, or until golden. Yields 10-12 muffins.

# baked apples

*¹/₂ cup raisins, chopped*
*6 small red apples*
*2 tablespoons butter, melted*
*2 tablespoons lemon juice*
*¹/₂ cup brown sugar*
*2 teaspoons cinnamon*
*1 cup water*

Place raisins in a dish of water to soak. Wash and core apples down to ¹/₂ inch at base. Mix together butter, lemon juice, brown sugar and cinnamon. Drain raisins and fold into mixture. Fill each apple cavity with the mixture, sprinkle tops of each apple with more cinnamon, and place in baking dish filled with water. Bake, covered, at 350 degrees for approximately one hour, or until tender. For better flavor, baste apples with juice during baking. Serves 6.

# Menu 8

spaghetti and meat sauce

tomato and artichoke salad

garlic toast

pound cake

The popularity of meals in our house is gauged by the number of drips and spots on the dog-eared recipe card. This spaghetti sauce (you should see the card!) is probably our family's favorite. I hope it will be yours, too.

# spaghetti and meat sauce

*1 pound ground beef*
*1 clove garlic, minced*
*One 15-ounce can tomato sauce*
*One 6-ounce can tomato paste*
*1 cup water*
*3 tablespoons dried onion flakes*
*2 teaspoons brown sugar*
*1¹/₂ teaspoons oregano*
*¹/₂ teaspoon basil*
*cooked spaghetti*

Brown ground beef with garlic and drain grease. Add
remaining ingredients and simmer for 1-2 hours. Serve
over cooked spaghetti. Meat sauce freezes well. Serves 6
to 8.

# tomato and artichoke salad

*One 8¹/₂-ounce can artichoke hearts, drained*
*3 tomatoes*
*¹/₂ cup purple onion, finely chopped*
*¹/₂ cup oil*
*¹/₄ cup wine vinegar*
*2 tablespoons chopped parsley*
*¹/₂ teaspoon oregano*
*¹/₂ teaspoon basil*
*¹/₂ teaspoon sugar*
*¹/₂ teaspoon salt*
*¹/₄ teaspoon pepper*

Slice artichoke hearts and tomatoes into bite-size pieces.
Combine remaining ingredients and pour over vegetables.
Chill and marinate overnight, or several hours. Drain and
serve on lettuce leaves. Serves 6.

# garlic toast

*1 loaf French bread*
*1 stick butter or margarine*
*¹/₂ teaspoon minced garlic*

Cut bread into thick slices and lay on cookie sheet. Place under oven broiler to toast. Combine butter and garlic over low heat until melted. Spread butter mixture on untoasted side and return to broiler until golden. Serve immediately. Serves 6 to 8.


# pound cake

*1¹/₂ cups butter, softened*
*2 cups sugar*
*7 egg yolks*
*3 cups flour*
*1 teaspoon baking powder*
*7 egg whites, beaten until fluffy*
*1 teaspoon vanilla*

Cream together butter and sugar with electric mixer, adding egg yolks. Sift together flour and baking powder and mix in. Fold into beaten egg whites and vanilla, and pour into greased tube pan. Bake at 350 degrees for one hour, or until inserted toothpick comes out clean. If desired, serve with fruit topping or whipped cream. Serves 10 to 12.

# Menu 9

veal cutlets

with mushroom sauce

green rice

stewed okra

marinated asparagus

bran muffins

cookies and cream frozen
dessert

# veal cutlets with mushroom sauce

*4 veal cutlets*
*1 cup flour*
*1 teaspoon salt*
*$1/2$ teaspoon pepper*
*1 egg, slightly beaten with 1 tablespoon water*
*1 cup bread crumbs*
*$1/4$ cup oil*

Pound cutlets to tenderize if desired. Roll in flour mixed with salt and pepper, then dip in egg mixture. Next, coat with bread crumbs and brown lightly in hot oil. Then cook slowly for 30 minutes. Serves 4.

*Mushroom Sauce:*
*2 tablespoons butter*
*2 tablespoons flour*
*1 cup light cream*
*$1/4$ teaspoon salt*
*$1/4$ teaspoon pepper*
*One $2^1/2$-ounce jar sliced mushrooms*

In small pan, melt butter and add flour. Stir in salt, pepper and cream, stirring continuously over medium heat until thick. Add mushrooms and serve warm with veal cutlets.

# green rice

*1 cup rice, cooked to yield 3 cups*
*1/4 cup chopped onion*
*1/2 cup grated cheese*
*1/2 cup chopped parsley*
*1/4 clove garlic, minced*
*1 egg, beaten*
*2 tablespoons butter, melted*
*1 cup milk*
*1 teaspoon salt*
*1/4 teaspoon pepper*

Combine all ingredients and place in greased casserole dish. Bake, covered, at 350 degrees for one hour. Serves 6 to 8.

# stewed okra

*2 cups okra, sliced*
*¹/₄ cup margarine*
*1 onion, chopped*
*1 green pepper, chopped*
*One 14-ounce can stewed tomatoes*
*1 teaspoon salt*
*¹/₄ teaspoon pepper*

Sauté okra in margarine. Add onion and pepper, cooking until tender. Stir in remaining ingredients, cover, and simmer for 45 minutes. Serves 6 to 8.

# marinated asparagus

*1 can asparagus spears*
*1 cup salad oil*
*¹/₃ cup sugar*
*4 tablespoons vinegar*
*1 teaspoon celery seed*
*1 teaspoon dry mustard*
*1 teaspoon salt*

Drain asparagus and place in shallow glass dish. Combine remaining ingredients and pour over asparagus. Cover and chill for at least one hour. Serves 4.

# bran muffins

1 egg
$^{1}/_{2}$ cup sugar
$^{1}/_{3}$ cup oil
1 cup milk
1 cup flour
2 teaspoons baking powder
$^{1}/_{2}$ teaspoon baking soda
$^{1}/_{2}$ teaspoon salt
2 cups bran cereal
$^{1}/_{2}$ cup raisins

Beat egg with fork, adding sugar, oil and milk. Sift together flour, baking powder, soda and salt, and combine with egg mixture. Fold in cereal and raisins and spoon into greased muffin cups, $^{2}/_{3}$ full. Bake at 400 degrees for 20-25 minutes. Yields 10-12 muffins.

# cookies and cream frozen desert

*½ pint whipping cream*
*½ cup sugar*
*1 half-gallon vanilla mellorine or ice cream, softened*
*16-ounce pkg. chocolate cream-filled sandwich cookies*

Whip cream with sugar, and add mellorine. Crush cookies and blend in. Spread into 9x12-inch pan. Wrap and freeze. Thaw for 15 minutes before slicing into squares for serving. Serves 10 to 12.

# Menu 10

baked fish

rice almondine

creamed spinach

cucumber salad

hard bakery rolls

coconut cream pie

The best part of church socials and pot-luck dinners was always the scrumptious dessert table. This menu includes a from-scratch coconut cream pie—guaranteed to bring the best of the dessert table into your kitchen.

# baked fish

*1 1/2 pounds fish fillets (sole is good)*
*4 lemons*
*1/2 cup butter, melted*
*salt*
*pepper*
*paprika*

Place the fish in a shallow, greased baking dish. Peel 2 lemons, slice thin and remove seeds. Place lemon slices over fish pieces. Pour butter over all, sprinkle with salt, pepper and paprika, and bake at 350 degrees for about 15 minutes, or until fish flakes. Cut remaining 2 lemons into wedges and serve with warm fish. Serves 4.

# rice almondine

*1 green pepper, chopped*
*1 onion, chopped*
*1 stick butter or margarine*
*1 cup long grain rice*
*One 10 1/2-ounce can condensed beef consomme*
*One 10 1/2-ounce can condensed beef bouillon*
*1/2 can water*
*One 4-ounce package sliced almonds*
*1 teaspoon salt*

Sauté green pepper and onion in butter. Add rice and cook until lightly browned. Combine with remaining ingredients and pour into greased baking dish. Bake, covered, at 350 degrees for one hour. Serves 6 to 8.

# creamed spinach

*¹/₃ stick butter or margarine*
*¹/₄ cup chopped onions*
*Two 10-ounce packages frozen spinach, thawed slightly*
*1¹/₂ teaspoons salt*
*1 cup sour cream*

Melt butter in heavy skillet. Add onion and cook until soft. Add spinach and cook for about 10 minutes. Stir in salt and sour cream and heat thoroughly. Serves 8.

# cucumber salad

*2 medium cucumbers*
*1 cup sour cream*
*1 tablespoon grated onion*
*1 tablespoon chopped parsley*
*1 teaspoon dill*
*1 teaspoon salt*

Peel and slice cucumbers. Mix together remaining ingredients and toss with cucumbers. Chill. Serves 6 to 8.

# coconut cream pie

*2 cups milk, divided*
*$1/4$ cup cornstarch*
*2 tablespoons butter*
*$3/4$ cup sugar*
*$1/2$ teaspoon salt*
*3 egg yolks, slightly beaten*
*1 teaspoon vanilla*
*One $3^1/2$-ounce can grated coconut*

Heat $1^1/2$ cups milk to scalding. Mix cornstarch with remaining $1/2$ cup of milk and combine with scalded milk, along with butter, sugar and salt. Add egg yolks and bring to a boil, stirring constantly. Continue stirring over moderate heat for two more minutes, until thick. Remove from heat and fold in vanilla and coconut (reserving $1/4$ cup coconut to sprinkle on meringue). Cool slightly and pour into baked 9-inch shell. Top with meringue. Serves 8.

*Meringue:*
*3 egg whites*
*$1/2$ teaspoon cream of tartar*
*$1/3$ cup sugar*

Beat egg whites and cream of tartar. Slowly add sugar and continue beating until stiff peaks form. Spread on pie and sprinkle with remaining coconut. Bake at 325 degrees for 15 minutes, until meringue is golden.

*Pie Crust:*
*1 cup all-purpose flour*
*1/2 teaspoon salt*
*1/3 heaping cup shortening*
*2 tablespoons ice water*

Sift together flour and salt in large mixing bowl, and with two knives or pastry blender, cut in shortening until grainy. Add the water and mix thoroughly. Knead lightly and roll out to circular shape on floured surface. Carefully fold pastry and place into 9-inch pie pan, crimping along edges. Prick surface lightly with a fork, and bake at 450 degrees for 9-11 minutes, until crust is golden and flaky. Bake before filling.

# Menu 11

beef stroganoff

with buttered noodles

glazed carrots

tomato aspic

bakery rolls

bread pudding

# beef stroganoff with buttered noodles

$1/2$ cup chopped onion
1 clove garlic, minced
1 cup sliced mushrooms
4 tablespoons butter
1 pound sirloin steak, cut into bite-size strips
$1/4$ cup flour
$1/2$ teaspoon salt
$1/4$ teaspoon pepper
2 tablespoons ketchup
$3/4$ cup beef broth or bouillon
1 cup sour cream

Sauté onion, garlic and mushrooms in butter in a large skillet, and remove to a warm plate. Coat steak strips with combined flour, salt and pepper. Brown beef over low heat in skillet. Then return onion-mushroom mixture to pan, and stir in ketchup and broth. Cover tightly and simmer for approximately one hour, adding water or more broth if necessary. Add sour cream and heat thoroughly. Serve hot over buttered noodles. Serves 4-6.

*Buttered Noodles:*
*One 8-ounce package wide egg noodles*
*3 tablespoons butter or margarine*
*1 tablespoon chopped parsley*

Cook noodles according to directions on package and drain. Gently fold in butter until it melts, and toss in parsley.

# glazed carrots

*6 medium carrots*
*4 tablespoons brown sugar*
*4 tablespoons butter or margarine*
*2 tablespoons orange juice*
*1 teaspoon lemon juice*
*¹/₄ teaspoon salt*

Peel and chop carrots and boil until tender. Drain. Mix together all other ingredients, add to carrots and heat together. Serves 4-6.

# tomato aspic

*4 cups tomato juice*
*3 tablespoons celery seed*
*¹/₄ cup minced onion*
*3 tablespoons sugar*
*1 tablespoon salt*
*¹/₂ cold water*
*2 envelopes unflavored gelatin*
*2 tablespoons vinegar*
*lettuce leaves*
*mayonnaise*
*fresh parsley*

In saucepan, combine tomato juice, celery seed, onion, sugar and salt, and bring to a boil. Reduce heat and simmer for a few minutes. In separate bowl, combine cold water with gelatin and let stand a few minutes. Pour tomato mixture through strainer into mixing bowl and add gelatin mixture, stirring until dissolved and well mixed. Stir in vinegar and pour into 6 greased dishes and chill in refrigerator until congealed. Serve on lettuce leaves and garnish with dabs of mayonnaise and sprigs of parsley. Serves 6.

# bread pudding

*4 tablespoons butter, melted*
*5 cups cubed French bread*
*3 cups milk*
*4 eggs, beaten*
*1/2 cup sugar*
*1 tablespoon vanilla*
*1 teaspoon cinnamon*
*1/2 teaspoon nutmeg*

Drizzle butter over cubed bread and place into greased baking pan. Scald milk and stir in eggs, sugar, vanilla, cinnamon and nutmeg. Pour over the bread, stirring gently to moisten and soak. Bake at 375 degrees for 30 minutes. Serve warm with bourbon sauce or sweetened whipped cream. Serves 6.

*Bourbon Sauce:*
*2 cups vanilla ice cream*
*1/2 cup milk*
*1 cup bourbon*

Mix in a blender until smooth. Serve over warm bread pudding.

# Menu 12

fried chicken

with cream gravy

mashed potatoes

green beans

cheese biscuits

apple pie

Treat yourself to this crispy fried chicken dinner—the ultimate in "nouvelle Grandma" cuisine.

# fried chicken with cream gravy

*1¹/₂ cups flour*
*1 teaspoon salt*
*¹/₄ teaspoon pepper*
*3-4 pounds chicken pieces*
*³/₄ cup milk*
*oil*

Mix together flour, salt and pepper in shallow dish and set aside. Dip chicken pieces first in milk, then in flour mixture. In large skillet, heat about ¹/₂ inch oil. Place chicken in hot oil, brown and turn. Cover pan and cook for 20 to 30 minutes longer. Remove chicken and drain, reserving oil and crust particles to use in gravy. Serves 6.

*Cream Gravy:*
*¹/₄ cup flour*
*¹/₄ cup chicken drippings and crust particles*
*¹/₂ teaspoon salt*
*¹/₄ teaspoon pepper*
*2 cups milk*

In same skillet, stir flour into drippings. Add salt and pepper, cooking over low heat until mixture is smooth. Pour in milk, stirring constantly until thick. Serve immediately.

# mashed potatoes

(See page 4.)

# green beans

*1 pound fresh green beans*
*3 slices bacon, chopped*
*1 teaspoon salt*

Cut ends off the beans and slice diagonally. Place in saucepan with enough water to cover and add bacon pieces and salt. Bring to a boil, cover and simmer for 20-30 minutes, until tender. Drain and add salt and pepper if desired. Serves 4-6.

# cheese biscuits

*3 cups biscuit baking mix*
*2 tablespoons butter or margarine, melted*
*1 cup milk*
*1 cup grated cheddar cheese*

Mix together baking mix, butter and milk until well blended. Add cheese and knead dough slightly. Roll out on a floured surface to about $1/2$-inch thickness. Cut out biscuits with $2^{1}/_{2}$-inch biscuit cutter or top of round juice glass. Place biscuits on ungreased baking sheet and bake at 450 degrees for 10-12 minutes, until golden brown. Yields approximately one dozen biscuits.

# apple pie

*pastry for 2-crust pie*
*²/₃ cup sugar*
*1¹/₂ tablespoons cornstarch*
*¹/₄ teaspoon salt*
*1 teaspoon cinnamon*
*¹/₄ teaspoon nutmeg*
*6 cups apples, peeled and thinly sliced*
*2 tablespoons lemon juice*
*2 tablespoons butter*

Carefully line a 9-inch pie pan with crust. Combine sugar, cornstarch, salt and spices, and gently fold into apples. Pour coated apples into crust, sprinkle with lemon juice and dot with butter. Cover with remaining crust. Crimp edges and slash top of crust evenly to vent. Bake at 425 degrees for 40-50 minutes until crust is golden brown. Serve warm with vanilla ice cream. Serves 8.

**Apple Pie continued**

*Pastry for 2-Crust Pie:*
*2 cups all-purpose flour*
*1 teaspoon salt*
*³/₄ cup shortening*
*5 tablespoons ice water*

Sift together flour and salt in mixing bowl, and with pastry blender or two knives cut in shortening until grainy. Add the water and mix thoroughly. Knead lightly and form into two balls of dough. Roll out each ball to circular shape on floured surface, yielding 2 crusts.

# Menu 13

corned beef and cabbage

scalloped potatoes

marinated carrots

bakery rye bread

cherry crisp

Have a yen for "real" food—something soulful and honest? This menu is robust, filling and a real treat for the meat-and-potatoes crowd.

# corned beef and cabbage

*4-pound corned beef brisket*
*3 medium onions, quartered*
*2 carrots, peeled and chopped*
*2 stalks celery, chopped*
*1 head green cabbage, cut in wedges*

Place brisket in large pot, covering with water. Add onions, carrots, and celery and bring to a boil. Cover and simmer 4-5 hours. Add cabbage wedges during last 30 minutes of cooking time. Drain and serve with horseradish sauce. Serves 8 to 10.

*Horseradish sauce:*
*1 cup sour cream*
*1/3 cup prepared horseradish*
*1/2 teaspoon lemon juice*

Blend together and chill.

# scalloped potatoes

*4 green onions, chopped*
*4 tablespoons butter or margarine*
*3 tablespoons flour*
*1 teaspoon salt*
*1/2 teaspoon pepper*
*1 1/2 cups milk*
*4 potatoes, cooked, peeled and thinly sliced*
*1 1/2 cups grated cheddar cheese*

Cook onions in butter. Add flour, salt and pepper, and mix well. Slowly add milk and continue stirring over medium heat until thickened. Remove from heat and add cheese. In a greased casserole, layer half of the potatoes, top with the sauce, then repeat. Bake at 350 degrees for 30 minutes. Serves 4-6.

# marinated carrots

*1 pound carrots, peeled and sliced*
*1 onion, sliced thin*
*1 green pepper, sliced in thin rings*
*One 10-ounce can condensed tomato soup*
*1 cup sugar*
*³/₄ cup vinegar*
*¹/₂ cup oil*
*1 teaspoon prepared mustard*
*¹/₂ teaspoon salt*
*¹/₄ teaspoon pepper*

Simmer carrots in small amount of water until tender. Drain and cool, then layer in salad bowl with onion and pepper rings. Combine remaining ingredients and pour over vegetables. Chill. Drain marinade prior to serving. Serves 6 to 8.

# cherry crisp

*1 stick butter or margarine, melted*
*1 1/2 cups brown sugar*
*1 cup flour*
*1/2 teaspoon baking powder*
*1/4 teaspoon baking soda*
*1/4 teaspoon salt*
*1 cup oatmeal*
*One 1-pound can cherry pie filling*

Cream together butter and brown sugar. Sift together flour, baking powder, soda and salt, and combine with butter mixture. Fold in oatmeal. Spread half of batter into greased 9x9-inch baking dish. Spread cherry filling on top, followed by remaining batter mixture. Bake at 350 degrees for 30 minutes. Serve warm with vanilla ice cream. Serves 6 to 8.

# Menu 14

stuffed green peppers with rice

cauliflower with cheese sauce

pineapple gelatin salad

herb bread

spice cake

A good rule of thumb is if you find that you're on a first-name basis with your pizza deliveryman, you're probably not cooking enough dinners at home!

# stuffed green peppers with rice

*4 medium or 6 small green peppers*
*¹/₂-pound ground chuck*
*1 onion, chopped*
*2 tablespoons butter*
*half of 10¹/₂-ounce can tomato soup*
*2 teaspoons Worcestershire sauce*
*1 teaspoon salt*
*¹/₄ teaspoon pepper*
*¹/₂ cup rice, cooked to yield 1¹/₂ cups*

Cut off tops and remove seeds from the peppers. Parboil for 5 minutes and drain. Cook beef and onion in butter until tender. Add ¹/₂ can of soup, Worcestershire sauce, salt and pepper. Fold in rice, mix well, and spoon mixture into peppers. Place filled peppers upright in casserole and add hot water to cover bottom of dish. Bake at 350 degrees for 30-45 minutes. During last 10 minutes of baking time, top with sauce. Serves 4.

*Sauce:*
*half of 10¹/₂-ounce can condensed tomato soup*
*1 teaspoon Worcestershire sauce*
*1 teaspoon prepared mustard*
*Mix together.*

# cauliflower with cheese sauce

*2 pounds cauliflower*

Remove leaves and separate into flowerets. Place in enough boiling, salted water to cover. Simmer, covered, for 15-20 minutes. Drain.

*Cheese Sauce:*
*2 tablespoons butter or margarine*
*2 tablespoons flour*
*1 cup milk*
*3/4 cup grated American cheese*
*1/2 teaspoon salt*

Melt butter and mix in flour. Add milk and cheese slowly, stirring constantly until thick. Fold in salt and serve warm over drained cauliflower. Serves 6.

# pineapple gelatin salad

*One 3-ounce package strawberry gelatin*
*1½ cups hot water*
*1 cup crushed pineapple*
*½ cup sugar*
*1 cup grated cheddar cheese*
*1 cup whipping cream, whipped*

In small saucepan over low heat, combine gelatin with hot water. Add pineapple and sugar and heat until sugar melts. Remove from stovetop, cool slightly and fold in cheese and whipped cream. Pour into shallow pan or mold, and refrigerate until set. Serves 6.

# herb bread

*1¹/₄ cups warm water*
*1 package dry yeast*
*3 tablespoons sugar*
*2 teaspoons salt*
*2 tablespoons butter, melted*
*3 teaspoons parsley*
*2 teaspoons chives*
*1 teaspoon dill*
*3³/₄ cups flour, divided*

Pour warm water into a large bowl and mix in yeast until it dissolves. Combine sugar, salt, butter, herbs and half of flour. Stir in yeast mixture. Beat two minutes at medium speed, adding remaining flour. Cover bowl and allow to rise for 30-45 minutes. Turn out onto flowered board and knead lightly for approximately five minutes. Gently pat into a greased 9x5 inch loaf pan. Cover and allow to rise for another hour. Bake at 350 degrees for 45-55 minutes or until lightly browned. Serves 6 to 8.

# spice cake

*1 cup butter, softened*
*2 cups sugar*
*5 eggs*
*1 cup buttermilk*
*3 cups all-purpose flour*
*1 teaspoon baking soda*
*1 tablespoon ground cloves*
*1 tablespoon cinnamon*
*1/2 teaspoon salt*
*1/2 cup confectioner's sugar*

Grease and flour a tube or bundt pan. With electric mixer, cream butter until fluffy. Add sugar, then eggs, one at a time. Add buttermilk. Sift together flour, soda, spices, and salt, and add to egg mixture, blending well. Pour into pan and bake at 350 degrees for 45-55 minutes, or until inserted toothpick is dry. Cool in pan for 30 minutes, then turn out onto serving plate. Sift confectioner's sugar on top of warm cake. Serves 10 to 12.

# Menu 15

chicken with mushroom sauce

wild rice

asparagus with lemon butter

orange-almond salad

bakery rolls

carrot cake

Do memories of your mom's cooking evoke feelings of love and security? Create memories for your family and start your own traditions with this "company chicken" for those special times.

# chicken with mushroom sauce

*6-8 deboned chicken breast halves*
*6-8 slices bacon*
*One 2$^1$/$_2$-ounce jar dried beef*
*1 cup sour cream*
*One 10$^1$/$_2$-ounce can condensed cream of mushroom soup*
*One 4-ounce jar sliced mushrooms, drained*

Wrap each piece of chicken with bacon. Line casserole dish with dried beef pieces. Mix sour cream, soup and mushrooms. Place chicken breasts on beef and spread soup mixture over all. Bake, uncovered, at 325 degrees for 1$^1$/$_2$ hours. Serves 6.

# wild rice

*4 cups water*
*1 teaspoon salt*
*1 teaspoon butter*
*1 cup wild rice*

In saucepan, bring water to a boil. Add salt, butter and rice, stirring well. Cover and reduce heat. Simmer for 35-45 minutes, or until all water is absorbed and rice is done. Serves 4.

# asparagus with butter sauce

*1 pound asparagus*
*$^{1}/_{2}$ cup melted butter*
*1 teaspoon lemon juice*
*$^{1}/_{4}$ teaspoon salt*

Cut off white ends of each asparagus spear. Tie loosely in a bunch, place in enough boiling salted water to cover, and cook uncovered for 15-20 minutes until tender.

In separate pan, combine butter, lemon juice and salt over low heat. Pour over drained asparagus. Serves 4.

# orange-almond salad

*8 cups shredded lettuce*
*Two 11-ounce cans mandarin oranges*
*1 cup slivered almonds*
*4-5 small green onions, chopped*

Toss together all ingredients and top with celery seed dressing. Serves 8 to 10.

*Celery Seed Dressing:*
*1 cup salad oil*
*1/3 cup vinegar*
*1/3 cup sugar*
*1/4 cup minced onion*
*1 tablespoon celery seeds*
*1 teaspoon dry mustard*
*1 teaspoon salt*

Mix together and chill.

# carrot cake

*1¹/₂ cups cooking oil*
*2 cups sugar*
*4 eggs*
*2 cups flour*
*2 teaspoons cinnamon*
*2 teaspoons soda*
*2 teaspoons baking powder*
*1 teaspoon vanilla*
*3 cups grated carrots*
*1 cup chopped pecans*

Beat oil and sugar well. Add eggs, one at a time, beating well after each addition. Sift together flour, cinnamon, soda and baking powder; blend with egg mixture. Fold in vanilla, carrots, and pecans. Bake in greased 9x13-inch pan at 325 degrees for one hour, or until done. Cool before topping with icing. Serves 8 to 10.

*Icing:*
*8 ounces cream cheese*
*¹/₂ stick margarine*
*One 1-pound box confectioner's sugar*

Cream cheese, margarine, and sugar until smooth.

# Menu 16

liver and onions

boiled new potatoes

green bean casserole

broiled tomatoes

angel biscuits

strawberry shortcake

Times change, but some recipes don't—and they shouldn't. This menu includes the traditional green-bean casserole, a classic that has graced American dinner tables for generations.

# liver and onions

*4 slices bacon*
*1 pound calf liver (¹/₂ inch thick)*
*1 cup flour*
*1 teaspoon salt*
*¹/₂ teaspoon pepper*
*1 onion, sliced thin*
*4 tablespoons butter*

Cook bacon, set aside and reserve grease. Cut liver into serving-size pieces and coat with flour mixed with salt and pepper. Cook liver in bacon grease until done, about 2 minutes on each side. At the same time, in a separate pan, sauté onion in butter until done. Spoon onion over liver pieces and crumble bacon on top. Serves 4.

# boiled new potatoes

*10-12 small new potatoes*
*6 tablespoons melted butter*
*parsley*

Scrub potatoes and cover with boiling, salted water. Cook, covered, for 45 minutes to an hour, or until tender. Serve warm with melted butter and a sprinkle of parsley. Serves 4-6.

# green bean casserole

*Two 16-ounce cans cut green beans, drained*
*One 8-ounce can sliced water chestnuts, drained*
*One 10¹/₂-ounce can condensed cream of mushroom soup*
*One 2.8-ounce can fried onion rings*

Mix together all ingredients, reserving some onion rings for topping. Place in greased casserole and bake at 350 degrees for 30-45 minutes. Serves 8.

# broiled tomatoes

*4 medium red tomatoes*
*2 tablespoons butter, melted*
*salt*
*pepper*
*¹/₄ cup finely ground bread crumbs*
*Parmesan cheese*

Cut tomatoes in half crosswise. Brush cut surface with butter. Sprinkle with salt, pepper, bread crumbs and Parmesan cheese, in that order. Place under preheated broiler for 1-2 minutes, or until lightly browned. Serves 8.

# angel biscuits

*1 package dry yeast*
*2 tablespoons warm water*
*2¹/₂ cups flour*
*¹/₂ teaspoon baking soda*
*1 teaspoon baking powder*
*1 teaspoon salt*
*2 tablespoons sugar*
*¹/₂ cup shortening*
*1 cup buttermilk*

Stir yeast into warm water until dissolved and set aside. Mix together dry ingredients in the order listed. Cut shortening in with pastry blender or two knives. Add buttermilk and yeast mixture, and blend thoroughly. Place in large, covered bowl in refrigerator and let rise for at least one hour. (Dough keeps well for several days in refrigerator.) When ready to bake, roll out on floured surface to ¹/₄ inch thickness, and cut with 2¹/₂-inch biscuit cutter or round juice glass. Place on greased cookie sheet and allow to rise slightly, approximately one hour. Bake at 425 degrees for 10-12 minutes. Yields approximately 2 dozen.

# strawberry shortcake

This is the old-fashioned shortcake recipe, but you can also serve shortcake the easy way by using slices of bakery angel-food cake instead.

*2 cups flour*
*4 teaspoons baking powder*
*1/2 teaspoon salt*
*1/4 cup sugar*
*1/2 cup butter*
*3/4 cup milk*
*1 quart fresh strawberries, sliced*
*1 cup heavy cream, sweetened and whipped*

Sift together flour, baking powder, salt and sugar. Using two knives, cut in butter until grainy. Stir in milk and form into dough. Roll out on floured board and cut with large, round cookie cutters (3-4 inches in diameter). Place rounds on ungreased cookie sheet and bake at 425 degrees for 12-15 minutes. Split shortcakes crosswise and fill with strawberries and whipped cream and top with same. Serves 6.

# Menu 17

chicken cacciatore

buttered noodles

baked acorn squash

broccoli salad

chess pie

# chicken cacciatore

*2-3 pounds chicken pieces*
*1 cup flour, seasoned with salt and pepper*
*1/2 cup olive oil*
*1 clove garlic, minced*
*Two 16-ounce cans stewed tomatoes*
*1 tablespoon chopped parsley*
*1 teaspoon oregano*
*1 1/4 teaspoon salt*
*1/2 teaspoon pepper*
*1/2 teaspoon basil*

Coat chicken pieces in flour mixture. Heat olive oil in large skillet and brown garlic and chicken pieces. Combine tomatoes and spices and pour over chicken. Cover and simmer for about 30 minutes, until chicken is tender, adding water to sauce if necessary. Serves 4-6.

# buttered noodles

*One 8-ounce package egg noodles*
*3 tablespoons butter or margarine*
*1 tablespoon chopped parsley*

Cook noodles according to directions on package and drain. Gently fold in butter until it melts and toss in parsley. Serves 4.

# baked acorn squash

*3 acorn squash*
*¹/₄ cup butter or margarine, melted*
*¹/₃ cup brown sugar*
*1 teaspoon cinnamon*
*¹/₂ teaspoon salt*
*¹/₂ teaspoon ginger*

Cut squash in half lengthwise and, with a spoon, scoop out interior strings and seeds. In baking pan with ¹/₂-inch hot water, place squash cut side down. Bake at 350 degrees for 30-40 minutes, until tender. Remove from oven and turn to cut side up. Combine remaining ingredients and pour inside squash. Return to oven for 15 minutes until glaze is golden. Serves 6.

# broccoli salad

*2 pounds fresh broccoli*
*1 cup mayonnaise*
*1 small onion, chopped*
*3 tablespoons vinegar*
*2 tablespoons sugar*
*1 teaspoon Worcestershire sauce*
*dash Tabasco*

Trim off broccoli stems and separate into flowerets. Combine remaining ingredients and pour over broccoli. Better if marinated 24 hours. Serves 6 to 8.

# chess pie

*1²/₃ cups sugar*
*1 tablespoon flour*
*1 tablespoon cornmeal*
*4 eggs*
*4 tablespoons butter, melted*
*4 tablespoons lemon juice*
*1 lemon rind, grated*
*1 unbaked 9-inch pie shell*

Mix together sugar, flour and cornmeal. Using electric mixer at medium speed, add the eggs one at a time. Mix in butter, lemon juice and rind until smooth. Pour into pie shell and bake at 375 degrees for 35 minutes, or until top is lightly browned. Serves 8.

For pie crust, see page 36.

# Menu 18

steak with butter sauce

twice baked potatoes

broccoli with hollandaise sauce

tossed green salad

crusty bakery rolls

quick chocolate cake

A great way to expand your recipe collection is through your extended family. We had a large family reunion one summer, and came away with a family reunion cookbook. It's an especially fun way to appreciate family ties throughout the year, as you serve "Aunt Dottie's chili" or "Grandma's chicken and dumplings."

# steak with butter sauce

*2 tablespoons butter*
*4 steaks, sirloin or strip,*
*approximately 8 ounces each, ³/₄-inch thick*
*salt*
*pepper*

On medium-high heat, melt butter and add steaks. Cook 5 minutes on each side for medium rare or 7 minutes on each side for well done. Salt and pepper to taste. Serve warm with butter sauce. Serves 4 to 6.

*Butter Sauce:*
*¹/₂ cup butter*
*2 tablespoons lemon juice*
*2 tablespoons parsley*

In small saucepan, melt butter. Remove from heat, and stir in lemon juice and parsley. Pour over warm steak.

# twice baked potatoes

*4 medium potatoes*
*1 cup sour cream*
*4 tablespoons butter or margarine, melted*
*1 teaspoon salt*
*1 teaspoon pepper*
*4 strips bacon, fried and crumbled*
*2-3 green onions, chopped*
*Parmesan cheese*
*paprika*

Bake potatoes until well done. Cut in half lengthwise; scoop out filling carefully, leaving skins intact. Using electric mixer, whip potatoes together with sour cream, butter, salt and pepper. Fold in bacon and onions. Heap the potato mixture back into shells and sprinkle liberally with Parmesan cheese, then paprika. Bake at 350 degrees for 15-20 minutes, until thoroughly heated. Yields 8 heaping potato halves.

# broccoli with
# hollandaise sauce

*2 pounds broccoli*

Pull off all leaves and outer skin on main stems, slicing large stems. Place in pan of boiling, salted water and cook uncovered for 20-30 minutes until tender. Drain and serve with hollandaise sauce. Serves 6 to 8

*Blender Hollandaise Sauce:*
*1/2 cup butter*
*3 egg yolks*
*2 tablespoons lemon juice*
*1/2 teaspoon salt*
*1/4 teaspoon cayenne pepper*

Heat butter until bubbling. Place egg yolks, lemon juice, salt and pepper in blender, and mix on low speed. Remove cover and pour in hot butter in steady stream, blending slowly Serve immediately. Yields 3/4 cup.

# tossed green salad

*1¹/₂ quarts mixed salad greens*
*One 6-ounce jar artichoke hearts, drained*
*2 medium tomatoes, cut into small wedges*
*1 avocado, peeled and sliced*
*1 cup croutons*

Mix together vegetables and toss. Sprinkle croutons on top. Serve with Thousand Island Dressing. Serves 8.

*Thousand Island Dressing:*
*1 cup mayonnaise*
*¹/₄ cup chili sauce*
*3 tablespoons chopped green olives (with pimiento)*
*1 tablespoon grated onion*
*1 teaspoon chopped parsley*
*Combine and chill.*

# quick chocolate cake

*2 cups flour*
*2 cups sugar*
*1 stick margarine*
*1 cup water*
*1/2 cup oil*
*3 1/2 tablespoons cocoa*
*1/2 cup buttermilk*
*2 eggs, beaten*
*1 teaspoon soda*
*1 teaspoon vanilla*

Combine flour and sugar, and set aside. In large saucepan, mix together margarine, water, oil and cocoa, and bring to a boil. Remove from heat and add flour mixture. Combine buttermilk, eggs, soda and vanilla, and mix in with other ingredients. Pour into greased 9x13-inch pan and bake for 20 minutes at 400 degrees. During last 5 minutes of cooking time, prepare icing in same saucepan. Serves 10 to 12.

**Quick Chocolate Cake continued**

*Icing:*
*1 stick margarine*
*3$\frac{1}{2}$ tablespoons cocoa*
*$\frac{1}{3}$ cup milk*
*One 1-pound box confectioner's sugar*
*One 3$\frac{1}{2}$-ounce can flaked coconut*
*1 cup chopped pecans*

Combine margarine, cocoa, and milk, and bring to a boil. Fold in sugar, coconut and nuts. Pour over warm cake, as soon as it is removed from the oven. Cool completely before cutting.

# Menu 19

lamb chops

noodles lorraine

harvard beets

wilted spinach salad

bakery rolls

chocolate cream pie

This old wives' tale still holds true—have a variety of colors, textures and shapes on your plate, and you're headed in the right direction nutritionally.

# lamb chops

*4 lamb chops*
*salt*
*pepper*
*mint jelly*

In hot, greased skillet, brown chops on each side to seal in juices. Continue cooking for about 10 minutes or until done, and season with salt and pepper. Serve with jelly.

# noodles lorraine

*One 8-ounce package wide noodles, cooked and drained*
*2 tablespoons butter*
*1 large onion, chopped*
*2 eggs, beaten*
*1 teaspoon salt*
*$^1/_2$ teaspoon nutmeg*
*4 slices bacon, cooked crisp and crumbled*
*2 cups grated Swiss cheese*
*$^1/_2$ cup grated Parmesan cheese*

Sauté onion in butter. In large bowl, combine all ingredients, carefully folding in noodles last. Place in greased baking dish and bake, covered, at 375 degrees for 45 minutes. Serves 6-8.

# harvard beets

*One 16-ounce jar of beets*
*2 tablespoons vinegar*
*2 tablespoons sugar*
*2 tablespoons butter, melted*
*2 tablespoons cornstarch*

Drain beets and set aside, reserving juice. Add water to juice to make one cup. Mix with vinegar, sugar, butter and cornstarch in small saucepan, and heat to boiling. Reduce heat and stir constantly as mixture thickens. Add beets and heat thoroughly. Serves 4.

# wilted spinach salad

*6 slices bacon*
*4 green onions, chopped*
*1/4 cup vinegar*
*1/4 cup water*
*4 teaspoons sugar*
*1 teaspoon salt*
*1/4 teaspoon pepper*
*8 cups torn spinach leaves*
*2 hard-cooked eggs, chopped*

Fry bacon until crisp. Remove from pan and crumble.
Add onion to pan drippings and sauté. Stir in vinegar,
water, sugar, salt, pepper and bacon pieces, and bring to
a boil. Pour hot dressing over spinach leaves. Toss and
sprinkle with chopped egg. Serves 8.

# chocolate cream pie

*4 egg yolks*
*2 cups milk*
*1 cup sugar*
*3 tablespoons cocoa*
*2 tablespoons cornstarch*
*1/2 teaspoon salt*
*4 tablespoons butter*
*1 teaspoon vanilla*
*9-inch baked pie shell*

In double boiler, mix eggs and milk over medium heat.
Sift together sugar, cocoa, cornstarch and salt, and add to
egg mixture. Stir constantly over heat until thick. Remove
from stovetop and fold in butter and vanilla, mixing well.
Cool slightly and pour into baked pie shell and chill.
Serve with sweetened whipped cream. For baked pie shell
recipe, see page 79. Serves 8.

# Menu 20

fried fish

with tartar sauce

french-fried potatoes

marinated vegetable salad

hush puppies

quick lemonade pie

# fried fish with tartar sauce

*2 pounds fish fillets (cod or flounder)*
*2 eggs, beaten with 1 teaspoon water*
*2 cups yellow cornmeal*
*1 teaspoon salt*
*¹/₄ teaspoon pepper*

Dip serving-size fish pieces first into egg mixture, then into cornmeal mixed with salt and pepper. Coat thoroughly and drop into preheated deep fryer of vegetable oil. Cook approximately 4 minutes or until golden brown. Serve with tartar sauce. Serves 4.

*Tartar Sauce:*
*1 cup mayonnaise*
*1 teaspoon prepared mustard*
*1 tablespoon minced onion*
*1 tablespoon sweet pickle relish*
*1 teaspoon chopped parsley*

Mix well and chill.

# french-fried potatoes

*6 large potatoes*
*salt*
*pepper*

Peel potatoes and rinse. Cut lengthwise into ½ inch slices.
Then cut each slice lengthwise into ½ inch strips. Cook
in preheated deep fryer of vegetable oil for 6 minutes or
more, until golden brown. Sprinkle with salt and pepper.
Serves 6 to 8.

# marinated vegetable salad

*1 can cut green beans, drained*
*1 can sliced water chestnuts, drained*
*1 can English peas, drained*
*1 cup thin-sliced celery*
*1 cup thin-sliced red onions*
*One 4-ounce jar pimientos*
*1 cup sugar*
*³/₄ cup cider vinegar*
*1 teaspoon salt*
*¹/₄ teaspoon pepper*

Combine first six ingredients in large bowl. Mix together remaining ingredients in small bowl and pour over vegetables. Cover and refrigerate at least four hours before serving. Can be kept several days in the refrigerator. Serves 6 to 8.

# hush puppies

*2 cups yellow cornmeal*
*1 tablespoon flour*
*1 teaspoon salt*
*1 teaspoon baking powder*
*$1/2$ teaspoon baking soda*
*3 tablespoons finely grated onion*
*1 cup buttermilk*
*1 egg, beaten*

Combine first five ingredients and stir in onion. Mix together buttermilk and egg, and stir into cornmeal mixture. Drop by tablespoonsful into hot grease, frying until golden brown. Drain and serve warm. Yields 2-3 dozen.

# quick lemonade pie

*One 6-ounce can frozen pink lemonade, thawed*
*One 14-ounce can sweetened condensed milk*
*One 15-ounce container prepared whipped topping*
*One 9-inch graham cracker crust*

Mix together lemonade, milk and whipped topping. Pour into crust and freeze. Thaw slightly before serving. Serves 8.

# *Menu 21*

chili con carne

avocado-grapefruit salad

quick cheese-biscuit bread

lemon bars

For a real '50s food fix, pour warm chili over a layer of corn chips. Sprinkle on chopped onion and grated cheddar cheese, and voila! Instant Frito Pie.

# chili con carne

*1¹/₂ cups dried pinto beans*
*2 tablespoons oil*
*1 clove garlic, minced*
*1 medium onion, chopped*
*1 small green pepper, chopped*
*1 pound chili meat or coarsely ground beef*
*Two 14-ounce cans tomatoes, chopped*
*2 tablespoons chili powder*
*1 teaspoon salt*
*1 teaspoon cumin*
*1 teaspoon pepper*

Cover beans with water and soak overnight. Cook in boiling, salted water until tender and drain. In hot oil, cook garlic, onion, green pepper and beef until browned. Drain grease. Add remaining ingredients and simmer for at least 2 hours, adding cooked beans to heat before serving. (Two 16-ounce cans of drained red kidney beans may be substituted for the dried beans.) Serves 8 to 10.

# avocado and grapefruit salad

*2 ripe avocados*
*1 large ripe grapefruit*
*lettuce leaves*
*French dressing*

Peel avocados and slice lengthwise. Peel grapefruit and separate into sections, removing skin. Alternate avocado and grapefruit sections on lettuce leaves. Pour French dressing over all. Serves 4.

# quick cheese-biscuit bread

*¹/₄ cup butter*
*¹/₂ teaspoon Worcestershire sauce*
*¹/₂ teaspoon dried onion flakes*
*¹/₄ teaspoon garlic salt*
*Two 7¹/₂-ounce cans refrigerated biscuits*
*¹/₂ cup grated cheddar cheese*

Melt butter and add Worcestershire sauce, onion flakes, and garlic salt over low heat, mixing well. Remove from heat. Dip each biscuit in butter mixture and sprinkle grated cheese on top. Place biscuits, overlapping and standing slightly upright, in greased round cake pan or 5¹/₂-inch ring mold. Bake at 400 degrees for 15-20 minutes. Serves 8.

# lemon bars

*Crust:*
*2 cups flour*
*2 sticks margarine, softened*
*$1/2$ cup powdered sugar*
*$1/4$ teaspoon salt*

*Filling:*
*4 eggs*
*2 cups sugar*
*$1/2$ cup lemon juice*
*$1/4$ cup flour*
*1 teaspoon baking powder*

*Topping:*
*1 cup powdered sugar*

Crust—Mix and press into 9 x 13-inch pan. Bake at 325 degrees for 15-20 minutes, until golden brown.

Filling—Beat eggs slightly. Add sugar, and juice. Sift together flour and baking powder and stir into egg mixture. Mix well and pour over baked crust. Bake at 325 degrees for 20-30 minutes. Remove and spread powdered sugar topping over warm cake. Cool completely and cut into squares. Serves 10 to 12.

# Menu 22

curried chicken

with white rice

red cabbage

bakery rolls

strawberry cloud

Little things can mean alot. Every now and then, make your mealtime a special occasion with your pretty linens, good dishes and silver, and candles. Memories are made of times like these.

# curried chicken with white rice

*¹/₂ cup butter or margarine*
*¹/₂ cup chopped onion*
*¹/₄ cup chopped celery*
*¹/₂ cup flour*
*2 teaspoons curry powder*
*1 teaspoon salt*
*2 cups cream*
*1¹/₂ cups chicken broth*
*3-4 cups cooked chicken, in bite-size pieces*
*¹/₂ cup chopped toasted almonds*
*3 cups steamed white rice*

Melt butter in large skillet. Add onion and celery, and cook until tender. Remove vegetables and stir flour, curry powder and salt into butter in pan. Add cream and chicken broth and bring to boil, stirring constantly until thick. Return vegetables to skillet and fold in chicken, heating thoroughly. Sprinkle almonds on top and serve over steamed white rice and with additional condiments, if desired. Serves 6 to 8.

*Optional condiments:*
*chutney*
*raisins*
*flaked coconut*

# red cabbage

*6 slices bacon, chopped*
*1 cup chopped onion*
*1 head red cabbage, shredded*
*1 apple, peeled and chopped*
*2 tablespoons brown sugar*
*1/4 cup vinegar*
*1 teaspoon salt*
*1/4 teaspoon pepper*

Fry bacon pieces until crisp. Remove bacon from pan and set aside. Saute onion in bacon grease until tender. Put cabbage in saucepan with 1/2 cup water, add bacon, onion and all other ingredients. Bring to a boil and simmer for 30 minutes, until tender. Serves 4-6.

# strawberry cloud

*6 tablespoons butter or margarine, melted*
*1½ cups graham cracker crumbs*
*One 3-ounce package strawberry gelatin*
*¾ cup boiling water*
*One 14-ounce can sweetened condensed milk*
*One 10-ounce package frozen sliced strawberries, thawed*
*1 cup whipping cream, whipped*

Combine butter with crumbs and press into bottom of 11x7-inch baking dish. Chill. In mixing bowl, combine gelatin with water until dissolved. Add milk and strawberries, then fold in whipped cream. Pour on top of crust and chill for 2-3 hours. Serves 6.

# Menu 23

pork chops

broccoli and rice casserole

applesauce salad

corn muffins

baked custard

# pork chops

*4 thick butterfly pork chops*
*$1/2$ cup orange juice*
*$1/2$ teaspoon curry powder*
*$1/2$ teaspoon dry mustard*
*$1/4$ teaspoon garlic powder*
*$1/4$ teaspoon salt*

Brown chops lightly on each side in greased skillet. Place in baking dish. Combine remaining ingredients and pour over chops. Bake, covered, at 350 degrees for one hour. Serves 4.

These are delicious when cooked in a crock pot. Cook on low heat for 7-9 hours, and they will be so tender.

# broccoli and rice casserole

*1 cup uncooked rice*
*¹/₄ cup butter margarine*
*¹/₂ cup chopped onion*
*One 10¹/₂-ounce can condensed cream of mushroom soup*
*One 10-ounce package frozen chopped broccoli, thawed*
*One 8-ounce jar processed American cheese*

Cook rice according to directions on box. Melt butter in skillet and sauté onion until done. Add soup, broccoli and cheese, and stir over low heat until cheese melts. Add cooked rice, mix well and pour into greased casserole dish. Bake at 325 degrees for 30 minutes. Serves 6.

# applesauce salad

*One 6-ounce package lemon gelatin*
*1/2 cup red cinnamon candies*
*3 cups boiling water*
*One 16-ounce jar applesauce*
*1 tablespoon lemon juice*
*lettuce leaves*
*mayonnaise*

Stir gelatin and candies into boiling water until dissolved. Fold in applesauce and lemon juice. Chill in 9x9-inch pan until set. Cut in squares and serve on lettuce leaves, topped with mayonnaise. Serves 6 to 8.

# corn muffins

*1 egg, beaten*
*½ cup oil*
*1 cup milk*
*1 cup flour*
*1 cup yellow cornmeal*
*1 tablespoon sugar*
*3 teaspoons baking powder*
*1 teaspoon salt*

In mixing bowl, use fork to beat egg with oil and milk. Sift together dry ingredients and stir into egg mixture. Pour into greased muffin cups, about ⅔ full. Bake at 425 degrees for 15-20 minutes. Serve immediately. Yields 10-12 muffins.

# baked custard

*2 cups milk*
*3 eggs, beaten*
*¼ cup sugar*
*¼ teaspoon salt*
*2 teaspoons vanilla*

In top of double boiler, scald milk. Combine eggs, sugar, salt and vanilla, and mix into milk. Pour into 4 custard cups and place in pan of hot water. Bake at 325 degrees for 30-45 minutes, or until inserted knife comes out clean. Serves 4.

CHINA

# Menu 24

beef stew

24-hour layered salad

cornbread

caramel-fudge brownies

When the weather gets cold, cloudy and dreary, a real "comfort" food is this very all-American beef stew.

# beef stew

*2¹/₂ - 3 pounds stew meat, cut into 1-inch pieces*
*¹/₂ cup oil*
*1 tablespoon salt*
*¹/₂ teaspoon pepper*
*1 cup chopped celery*
*1 cup chopped green pepper*
*1 cup chopped onion*
*One 14-ounce can stewed tomatoes*
*One 10-ounce can beef broth*
*One 6-ounce can tomato paste*
*¹/₂ cup water*
*¹/₄ teaspoon thyme*
*1 bay leaf*
*3 medium potatoes, peeled and chopped*
*4 carrots, chopped*

In large pot or Dutch oven, brown meat in hot oil. Remove from pan and sprinkle with salt and pepper. Add celery, green pepper and onion, and cook until tender. Drain grease. Combine tomatoes, broth, tomato paste, water and thyme, and stir into vegetable mixture, along with browned beef. Insert bay leaf and bring to a boil. Reduce heat and simmer, covered, for one hour, adding water as needed. Add potatoes and carrots, and continue cooking for another 1¹/₂ hours, or until tender. Serves 8 to 10.

*Beef Stew continued*

The stew adapts very well to the crock pot. Brown meat in oil, place all ingredients in pot at once, and reduce liquids by one-half. Cook on low heat for 10-12 hours.

# 24-hour layered salad

*1 large head iceberg lettuce, shredded*
*2 cups mushroom slices*
*1 large red onion, sliced*
*One 16-ounce can green peas*
*¼ pound grated Swiss cheese*
*2 cups mayonnaise*
*1 teaspoon sugar*
*1 teaspoon curry powder*
*4 slices bacon, cooked and crumbled*

In large salad bowl or deep dish, layer first five ingredients in order. Combine mayonnaise, sugar and curry powder, and spread over salad to seal. Top with crumbled bacon. Cover and refrigerate overnight before serving. Serves 8 to 10

# cornbread

(See page 30.)

# caramel-fudge brownies

*50 chewy caramel candies*
*¹/₃ cup evaporated milk*
*1 package German chocolate cake mix*
*³/₄ cup butter, softened*
*1 cup chopped pecans*
*¹/₃ cup milk*
*One 12-ounce package chocolate chips*

Combine caramels and evaporated milk in double boiler, stirring over medium heat until melted. Set aside. Grease and flour 8x12-inch pan. Combine remaining ingredients, except chocolate chips, to form dough. Press half of dough mixture in pan. Bake at 350 degrees for 6 minutes. Sprinkle chocolate chips over crust. Dot and spread melted caramel over chips. (It won't cover completely.) Spread remaining dough over caramel. Return to oven for 15-20 minutes or until done. Cool completely before cutting into squares. Serves 10 to 12.

# *Menu 25*

salmon croquettes

potato squares

pea salad

buttery bread sticks

chocolate ice cream pie

# salmon croquettes

*One16-ounce can salmon*
*1 egg, beaten*
*1 cup flour*
*$^1/_8$ teaspoon pepper*
*$1^1/_2$ teaspoons baking powder*

Drain salmon, reserving liquid. Remove bones from salmon.Blend in egg with fork, mixing well. Add flour and pepper. Measure $^1/_4$ cup salmon liquid and stir in baking powder, causing liquid to foam. When foaming stops, fold into salmon mixture. Drop by teaspoonsful into deep fryer of hot oil. Fry and turn, browning on all sides. Serves 4.

# potato squares

6 medium potatoes
2 cups sour cream
1 cup grated cheddar cheese
6 green onions, sliced
3 tablespoons milk
1 teaspoon salt
$^1/_2$ teaspoon pepper
3 teaspoons butter, melted
$^1/_2$ cup bread crumbs

Boil potatoes in jackets. Cool completely. Peel and grate.
Combine sour cream, cheddar cheese, onions, milk, salt
and pepper. Fold into grated potatoes and mix well. Spread
into 9x13-inch greased baking dish. Mix together butter
and bread crumbs and sprinkle on top. Bake at 300 degrees for 45 minutes. Cool slightly and cut into squares.
Serves 8-10.

# pea salad

*Two 10-ounce packages frozen green peas*
*1 cup sour cream*
*$^1/_2$ cup mayonnaise*
*$^1/_2$ cup cubed American cheese*
*3-4 green onions, chopped*
*1 teaspoon dill weed*
*1 teaspoon salt*
*$^1/_2$ teaspoon pepper*

Cook peas according to package directions, reducing cooking time by one half. Drain and cool. Combine remaining ingredients and fold in cooled peas. Chill. Serves 8.

# buttery bread sticks

*1 stick butter*
*2 cups biscuit baking mix*
*1 tablespoon sugar*
*$^1/_2$ cup milk*

Place butter in shallow baking dish and melt in oven. In mixing bowl, stir together biscuit mix and sugar. Then add milk, beating well with a spoon. Knead dough slightly on floured surface, and roll out to rectangle. Cut into strips and roll each one in pan of butter, coating all sides. Allow bread sticks to remain in buttered pan and bake at 425 degrees for 10-12 minutes, until golden brown. Yields 2 dozen.

# chocolate ice cream pie

*2 cups crispy rice cereal*
*$^1/_2$ cup white corn syrup*
*$^1/_2$ cup smooth peanut butter*
*1 quart chocolate ice cream, softened*

Mix together crispy rice cereal, corn syrup and peanut butter and pat into greased 9-inch pie pan to form crust. Spoon softened ice cream into crust. Cover well with waxed paper and freeze. Thaw slightly before slicing and serving. Serves 8.

# Menu 26

lasagna

baked zucchini

italian salad

italian cheese bread

cherry cheesecake

Many dishes, like this lasagna, can be made ahead of time and frozen. A timesaver that's worked well for me is getting together periodically with a group of friends for a "cooking party." We each bring ingredients for a recipe or two. One chops and stirs, one cleans up, one watches the kids, and we leave with an assortment of freezer-ready meals.

# lasagna

10 ounces lasagna noodles
1 pound grated mozzarella cheese
Parmesan cheese

Meat Sauce:
1 pound Italian sausage or ground beef
1 clove garlic, minced
1 teaspoon oregano
1 teaspoon basil
One 1-pound can tomatoes
Two 6-ounce cans tomato paste

Cheese Filling:
3 cups ricotta cheese
$^{1}/_{2}$ cup Romano cheese, grated
2 tablespoons parsley flakes
2 beaten eggs
2 teaspoons salt
$^{1}/_{2}$ teaspoon pepper

Brown meat slowly and drain grease. Add remaining meat sauce ingredients and simmer for 30 minutes, stirring occasionally. Cook noodles in boiling water according to package directions. Drain and rinse. Combine cheese filling ingredients. Layer the following in 9x13-inch pan: one-half of the noodles, ¹/₂ of cheese filling, ¹/₂ of grated mozzarella and ¹/₂ of meat sauce. Repeat. Sprinkle top liberally with Parmesan cheese. Bake at 375 degrees for 30 minutes. Can be frozen. Serves 10.

# baked zucchini

*3 medium zucchini*
*2 tablespoons butter or margarine, melted*
*garlic salt*
*Parmesan cheese, grated*

Trim ends of zucchini. Cut in half lengthwise, then crosswise. Place zucchini, cut side up, in greased baking dish and brush with melted butter. Sprinkle lightly with garlic salt then very generously with Parmesan cheese. Bake at 375 degrees for 30-45 minutes, until tender. Serves 6.

# italian salad

*1¹/₂ quarts mixed salad greens*
*¹/₄ cup anchovies*
*¹/₄ cup sliced black olives*
*¹/₄ cup chopped sweet Italian peppers*
*¹/₄ cup green pepper slices*

Toss and serve with vinaigrette dressing. Serves 8.

*Vinaigrette Dressing:*
*1 cup salad oil*
*¹/₃ cup sugar*
*4 tablespoons vinegar*
*1 teaspoon celery seeds*
*1 teaspoon dry mustard*
*1 teaspoon salt*
*1 clove garlic*

Mix together and chill. Remove garlic clove before serving.

# italian cheese bread

*1 loaf of French or Italian bread*
*1 stick butter or margarine, softened*
*$^{1}/_{2}$ cup Parmesan cheese, grated*
*3 tablespoons chopped parsley*
*$^{1}/_{2}$ teaspoon garlic powder*
*$^{1}/_{2}$ teaspoon oregano*
*$^{1}/_{2}$ teaspoon salt*

Make slices in loaf, not cutting all the way through. Mix together remaining ingredients until smooth and spread between bread slices. Wrap in foil and bake at 400 degrees for 15-20 minutes. Serves 6 to 8.

# cherry cheesecake

*Crust:*
*1¹/₂ cups graham cracker crumbs*
*¹/₂ cup butter, melted*
*3 tablespoons sugar*

*Filling:*
*5 eggs*
*Three 8-ounce packages cream cheese, softened*
*1¹/₂ cups sugar*
*2 tablespoons vanilla*

Mix together the graham cracker crumbs, butter, and sugar and press into the bottom of a 9-inch spring form pan. Beat eggs and add cream cheese, sugar, and vanilla, mixing until smooth. Pour into pan, on top of crust, and bake at 350 degrees for one hour. Let cake cool in pan, remove sides and transfer to serving plate. Top with cherry glaze. Serves 8.

### Cherry Cheesecake continued

*Cherry Glaze:*
*One 16-ounce can pitted tart cherries*
*1 cup sugar*
*3 tablespoons cornstarch*

Drain cherries and set aside, pouring juice into saucepan. Stir sugar and cornstarch into cherry juice and bring to a boil, stirring until thick. Fold in cherries and cook for a few minutes. Let cool and spread on cheesecake. Chill before serving.

# Menu 27

cheesy chicken and noodles

curried english peas

cherry pecan salad

angel biscuits

apple cake

This chicken casserole uses Velveeta—the cheese of choice around our house. I realized I'd had a retro transformation after becoming a mom, when instead of preparing baked brie for afternoon hors d'oeuvres, I found myself serving plates of sliced Velveeta with Ritz crackers!

# cheesy chicken and noodles

*8-ounce package wide egg noodles*
*1 onion, chopped*
*2 cups sliced mushrooms*
*¼ cup butter or margarine*
*Two 10½-ounce cans condensed cream of chicken soup*
*½ cup milk*
*2 cups grated processed American cheese*
*½ cup grated Parmesan cheese*
*One 16-ounce carton cottage cheese*
*4 chicken breast halves, cooked and shredded*

Cook noodles approximately 5 minutes. Sauté onion and mushrooms in butter. In large bowl, combine all ingredients, carefully folding in cooked noodles last. Pour into 10x14-inch pan and sprinkle liberally with more Parmesan cheese. Bake at 350 degrees for 45 minutes. Freezes well. Serves 8.

# curried english peas

*4 tablespoons butter*
*One 6-ounce can peanuts*
*1 teaspoon curry powder*
*2 cans English peas, drained*

Melt butter in skillet and stir in remaining ingredients until heated. Serves 6.

# cherry pecan gelatin salad

*One 6-ounce package cherry gelatin*
*One 16-ounce can pitted tart cherries, drained*
*1 cup chopped pecans*
*One 8-ounce package whipped cream cheese, softened*
*1 cup sour cream*
*1 tablespoon sugar*
*lettuce leaves*

Prepare gelatin according to package directions and pour into 13x9-inch baking pan, chilling in refrigerator for one hour. After mixture begins to set, stir in cherries and pecans. When totally set, mix together cream cheese, sour cream, and sugar and spread on top. Cut into squares and serve on a lettuce leaves. Serves 8.

# angel biscuits

(See page 137.)

# apple cake

*2 eggs*
*2 cups sugar*
*1¼ cups oil*
*3 cups flour*
*1 teaspoon salt*
*1 teaspoon baking powder*
*1 teaspoon cinnamon*
*2 teaspoons vanilla*
*3 cups diced apples*
*2 cups chopped walnuts*

Beat eggs, and mix in sugar and oil. Sift together flour, salt, baking powder and cinnamon, and add to egg mixture, mixing well. Fold in vanilla, apples, and nuts, and pour into greased and floured tube or bundt pan. Bake at 350 degrees for 65 to 75 minutes, or until done. Remove from pan and top with orange glaze. Serves 10 to 12.

*Orange Glaze:*
*1 cup powdered sugar*
*3 tablespoons orange juice*

Mix together and pour over warm cake.

# Menu 28

shrimp creole

with white rice

baked artichoke hearts

ambrosia

hard bakery rolls

pineapple upside down cake

We all need a home-cooked meal sometimes and whipping up old favorites in the kitchen can be absolutely therapeutic. After all, they don't call it comfort food for nothing!

# shrimp creole with white rice

*¹/₄ cup butter or margarine*
*1 cup chopped onion*
*¹/₂ cup chopped green pepper*
*¹/₂ cup chopped celery*
*1 clove garlic, minced*
*One 28-ounce can tomatoes*
*One 8-ounce can tomato sauce*
*1 teaspoon salt*
*1 teaspoon sugar*
*¹/₄ teaspoon paprika*
*3 drops red pepper sauce*
*1 pound cooked shrimp*
*3 cups steamed white rice*

Melt butter in saucepan. Add onion, green pepper, celery and garlic, and cook until tender. Add remaining ingredients, except shrimp and rice, and bring to a boil. Reduce heat and simmer at least 30 minutes, or longer if possible. Add cooked shrimp and heat thoroughly. Serve over steamed white rice. Serves 4-6.

# baked artichoke hearts

*1 cup bread crumbs*
*1 cup grated Parmesan cheese*
*¹/₂ bottle Italian dressing*
*Two 8¹/₂-ounce cans artichoke hearts, drained*

Combine crumbs, cheese and dressing. Place artichoke hearts in baking dish and pour crumb mixture over. Bake at 325 degrees for 20 minutes. Serves 6-8.


# ambrosia

*3 oranges*
*2 bananas*
*1¹/₂ cups flaked coconut*
*¹/₄ cup confectioner's sugar*

Peel and slice fruit into serving pieces, and arrange in bowl. Combine coconut and sugar, and pour over top. Chill. Serves 4.

# pineapple upside down cake

*Pineapple Mixture:*
*One 1-pound can sliced pineapple*
*¹/₂ cup butter or margarine, softened*
*²/₃ cup brown sugar*
*¹/₂ cup flaked coconut*

Drain pineapple, reserving 2 tablespoons juice. Cut pineapple slices in quarters. Mix together butter and brown sugar. Spread on bottom of 9-inch square baking pan. Sprinkle the reserved juice over it. Then arrange pineapple on top. Sprinkle with coconut.

*Batter:*
*2 cups sifted cake flour*
*¹/₄ teaspoon salt*
*2 teaspoons baking powder*
*¹/₂ cup shortening*
*1 cup sugar*
*1 egg*
*³/₄ cup milk*
*1 teaspoon vanilla*

### *Pineapple Upside Down Cake continued*

Sift together the flour, salt and baking powder. Cream the shortening; gradually beat in the sugar until light and fluffy. Beat in the egg. Add the flour mixture alternately with the milk, beating until blended. Add the vanilla and pour into prepared pan. Bake at 350 degrees for 45 minutes. Cool for five minutes and invert on serving dish, leaving pan on cake for a few minutes before removing. Serves 6 to 8.

# Menu 29

oven barbecued spareribs

potato salad

coleslaw

corn on the cob

garlic toast

pecan pie

# oven barbecued spareribs

*4 pounds spareribs*
*1 tablespoon salt*
*1 teaspoon pepper*

Cut ribs into serving-size pieces, and rub with salt and pepper. Place in shallow roasting pan with meat side up and roast at 350 degrees for 30 minutes. Pour barbecue sauce over ribs and continue baking for 1½ hours, basting several times. Serves 4 to 6.

*Barbecue Sauce:*
*2 cans tomatoes, chopped fine*
*2 cans water*
*½ clove garlic, minced*
*¼ cup vinegar*
*2 tablespoons powdered cumin*
*1 tablespoon sugar*
*1 teaspoon black pepper*
*2 large onions, diced*
*One 5-ounce bottle Worcestershire sauce*
*¼ cup ketchup*
*1 tablespoon prepared mustard*
*1 teaspoon cayenne pepper*
*1 pound margarine*

Mix together, bring to a boil, and simmer for at least one hour, or longer if possible.

# potato salad

4 medium potatoes, cooked, peeled and diced
1 teaspoon salt
$^1/_2$ teaspoon pepper
$^3/_4$ cup mayonnaise
1 teaspoon prepared mustard
1 cup chopped celery
$^1/_2$ cup sweet pickle relish
One 2-ounce jar diced pimientos
2 hard-cooked eggs, chopped

Salt and pepper potatoes. Combine remaining ingredients and fold into potatoes, adding more mayonnaise if desired. Chill. Serves 8 to 10.

# coleslaw

1 small head cabbage
2 medium carrots
1 medium bell pepper
$^3/_4$ cup mayonnaise
3 tablespoons milk
2 tablespoons vinegar
1 teaspoon celery seeds
2 teaspoons sugar
$^1/_2$ teaspoon salt

Shred cabbage and grate carrots. Chop bell pepper into small, thin strips. Combine remaining ingredients and pour over vegetables. Mix well, cover and chill. Serves 10 to 12.

# corn on the cob

*4 medium-sized ears of yellow corn*
*salt*
*pepper*
*butter*

Remove husks and cornsilk. Cut off tips of cobs. Place in enough unsalted boiling water to cover and cook, covered, for 10 minutes, or until tender. Drain and serve warm with salt, pepper, and butter. Serves 4.

# garlic toast

(See page 69 .)

# pecan pie

*3 eggs*
*1 cup light corn syrup*
*1 cup brown sugar*
*3 tablespoons butter*
*$^{1}/_{2}$ tablespoon flour*
*$^{1}/_{4}$ teaspoon salt*
*1 teaspoon vanilla*
*1 cup chopped pecans*
*1 unbaked 9-inch pie shell*
*1 cup pecan halves*

Preheat oven to 400 degrees. Beat eggs, adding syrup, sugar, butter, flour and salt. Fold in vanilla and 1 cup chopped pecans. Pour into unbaked pie shell, and place 1 cup pecan halves on top of batter. Reduce oven temperature to 350 degrees, and bake 40-50 minutes, or until filling is set. Serves 8.

For pie crust, see page 36 .

# Menu 30

chicken and dumplings

frozen fruit salad

banana nut bread

rice pudding

Research confirms what we've known all along—that there is a food-mood connection. When we're feeling tired or down in the dumps, for example, we often crave mushy, easy-to-chew foods. This chicken-and-dumplings menu is perfect for one of those days, when we're longing for the comfort and security of our childhood.

# chicken and dumplings

*4 pounds chicken pieces*
*1 small onion, chopped*
*1 clove garlic, minced*
*4 chicken bouillon cubes*
*1 bay leaf*
*1 stalk celery with leaves, chopped*
*1 teaspoon salt*
*$^{1}/_{2}$ teaspoon pepper*

Place chicken in enough water to cover in large pot. Bring to a boil and add other ingredients, simmering for about one hour, or until chicken is completely cooked. Remove chicken from broth, cool enough to debone pieces and keep broth simmering.

*Dumplings:*
*2 cups flour*
*1 teaspoon baking powder*
*$^{1}/_{2}$ cup hot chicken broth*
*1 teaspoon salt*
*$^{1}/_{3}$ cup shortening*

Sift dry ingredients together; cut in shortening. Add enough of the chicken broth to make a stiff dough. Roll dough out on a floured surface to $1/8$-inch thickness, and cut into 1"x4" strips and drop one at a time into the boiling broth. Reduce heat and return chicken to the pot, cooking until dumplings are done, 10-20 minutes. Stir gently during cooking to keep dumplings from sticking. Serves 6.

# frozen fruit salad

*One 3-ounce package cream cheese*
*2 tablespoons sour cream*
*$1/3$ cup mayonnaise*
*2 tablespoons lemon juice*
*2 tablespoons sugar*
*$1/8$ teaspoon salt*
*One 8-ounce can crushed pineapple*
*One 11-ounce can mandarin oranges, drained*
*$1/2$ cup chopped maraschino cherries*
*$1/2$ cup chopped pecans*
*1 cup heavy cream, whipped*
*lettuce leaves*

*Frozen Fruit Salad continued*

Blend together cream cheese, sour cream and mayonnaise. Add lemon juice, sugar and salt. Fold in fruits, nuts and cream, and pour into greased mold or shallow dish. Wrap well and freeze. To serve, thaw slightly before slicing and place on lettuce leaves. Serves 6-8.

# banana nut bread

*2 eggs*
*1 1/2 cups sugar*
*1/2 cup oil*
*1/4 cup buttermilk*
*2 cups flour*
*1 teaspoon soda*
*1 teaspoon salt*
*3 ripe bananas, mashed*
*1 cup chopped nuts*

Beat eggs and add sugar, oil and buttermilk. Sift together flour, soda and salt, and combine with egg mixture. Fold in bananas and nuts, and pour into two greased 9x5-inch loaf pans. Bake at 350 degrees for 50-60 minutes, or until inserted toothpick comes out clean.

# rice pudding

*3 eggs*
*2¹/₂ cups milk*
*²/₃ cup sugar*
*1 teaspoon vanilla*
*¹/₃ cup raisins*
*³/₄ cup white rice, cooked to yield about 2 cups*
*cinnamon*
*nutmeg*

Beat eggs. Add milk, sugar and vanilla. Fold in raisins and rice, and pour into buttered casserole. Place casserole in shallow pan of water and bake at 350 degrees for 35-45 minutes, or until set. Serve warm with a sprinkle of cinnamon and nutmeg on top. Serves 6.

# Menu 31

beans and franks

macaroni salad

small french bakery loaves

snickerdoodle cookies

Why the surge of popularity for traditional "mom's meals?"
Maybe it has a lot to do with our fast-paced and ever-changing
lives. What a great feeling to be able to come home to honest,
comforting food, and to know that some things can stay the
same.

# beans and franks

*2 onions, chopped*
*1 green pepper, chopped*
*½ cup butter or oil*
*Two 21-ounce cans pork and beans*
*1 cup ketchup*
*3 tablespoons vinegar*
*3 tablespoons brown sugar*
*1 tablespoon prepared mustard*
*1 tablespoon Worcestershire sauce*
*10-12 frankfurters, sliced*

Sauté onions and peppers in oil until tender. Drain grease, and mix together with remaining ingredients, except franks. Pour into greased casserole and top with frankfurter pieces. Bake, covered, at 350 degrees for 45 minutes, removing cover for last 15 minutes. Serves 6.

# macaroni salad

1 cup elbow macaroni
1 tablespoon oil
2 tablespoons vinegar
$^1/_2$ cup chopped celery
$^1/_2$ cup cubed American cheese
$^1/_2$ cup chopped stuffed olives
2 green onions, chopped
2 tablespoons chopped parsley
1 teaspoon salt
$^1/_4$ teaspoon pepper
3 tablespoons mayonnaise
lettuce leaves

Cook macaroni according to package directions. Toss with oil and vinegar. Add remaining ingredients, except lettuce, and chill. Serve on lettuce leaves. Serves 6 to 8.

# snickerdoodle cookies

*¹/₂ cup butter or margarine, softened*
*²/₃ cup sugar*
*1 egg*
*1¹/₂ cups all-purpose flour*
*¹/₂ teaspoon baking soda*
*¹/₄ teaspoon salt*
*¹/₂ teaspoon cream of tartar*
*1 teaspoon vanilla*
*2 tablespoons sugar mixed with 2 teaspoons cinnamon*

Beat together butter and sugar. Then add in egg. Sift together flour, soda, salt and cream of tartar, and combine with egg mixture. Fold in vanilla. Form dough into small balls, approximately 1 inch diameter. Roll in cinnamon and sugar mixture. Place balls approximately 2 inches apart on greased cookie sheet and bake at 375 degrees for 8-10 minutes. Yields 2-3 dozen cookies.

# Index

## breads

angel biscuits, 137

banana nut bread, 243

blueberry muffins, 61

bran muffins, 76

buttermilk biscuits, 22

buttery bread sticks, 204

cheese biscuits, 101

cheese-biscuit bread, quick, 173

cornbread dressing, 30-31

corn muffins, 188

garlic toast, 69

herb bread, 120

hush puppies, 167

Italian cheese bread, 212

popovers, 52

poppyseed bread, 44

*Breads continued*

refrigerator yeast rolls, 13

whole wheat rolls, 5

## desserts

ambrosia, 228

apple cake, 221

apple pie, 102-03

apples, baked, 62

banana pudding, 6

bananas foster, family-style, 45

Boston cream pie, 14-15

bread pudding, 94

brownies, caramel-fudge, 197

carrot cake, 130

cherry cheesecake, 213-14

cherry crisp, 112

chess pie, 144

# main dishes

# Notes